CAN YOU TELL A LIE?

The Power of Business Ethics

*"... knowledge without integrity
is dangerous and dreadful."*
Samuel Johnson, 1759

Louis N. Strike

"Words to live by, certainly, for all of us."

Frederick Russ, Ph.D., University of Cincinnati
Dean of the College of Business Administration

Publisher: Louis N. Strike
Production Editor/Designer: Holly Terry
Word Processing: Monica Pieper and Shawne Appel

Note: This book was originally published in 1997 as The Power of Business
Ethics. Because of the popularity of the first chapter, it has been renamed:
Can You Tell A Lie? The Power of Business Ethics.

Printed in the United States of America

ISBN No. 0-9665377-1-8

This book is dedicated to
those looking for a way
to do the right thing!

Acknowledgements

A special thank you to Chris Allen, Professor of Marketing, and Bob Faaborg, Professor of Philosophy — both from the University of Cincinnati — whose questioning required me to get this material organized and down on paper!

Who is Louie Strike?

Louie Strike has more than twenty years experience as a CEO; he earned his MBA at the University of Chicago and is a CPA with extensive commercial bank lending experience.

Specialization: Crisis management, profit improvement, risk reduction; turnarounds, reorganizations and the development of exit strategies; acquisitions, creative financing; as well as international business; firms with sales of $4,000,000 to $100,000,000 annually, private and public.

Industry Expertise: *Manufacturing:* automotive; machine tools; food processing; packaged goods; and architectural products. *Wholesale Distribution:* food service and retail groceries. *Other:* banking; insurance; finance companies; real estate; healthcare; and government contracting.

Previous Experience: CEO of Modernfold, Inc., North America's leading producer of operable walls; CEO of Cinpac, Inc., a defense contractor for MREs (food processing and packaged goods); Chairman of Libby Lee Toys; CEO of Lodge & Shipley, Inc. (machine tools and packaging equipment); CFO, COO and CEO of The Hess & Eisenhardt Manufacturing Company (automotive); Second Vice President, Continental Bank of Chicago (now Bank of America), managing a $400,000,000 business loan portfolio.

Professional Certification: Certified Public Accountant

Education: MBA: The University of Chicago
BA in Mathematics: The University of Utah
BA in Philosophy: The University of Utah

Author: *The Power of Business Ethics*
Predicting Bankruptcy & Eight Principles of Strategy
Wizard of Oz Management
"California Needs TVA-Type Power Plan" –
The Los Angeles Business Journal

Table of Contents

The Elements of Great Leadership • The Foundation
Statement of Ethics • The Problem of Scale • The
Assessment Questions of Business Ethics • Contracts and
Related Issues

The White Lie • Conflicts of Interest • Intuition • The
Ethical Dilemma

Ethics And The Business Leader • The Nexus of Business
Contracts • The Flow of Cash • The Conflict of Interest
Principle • The Stages of Negotiation • The World's

Introduction

My perspective on business ethics is one of a middle-market CEO. The middle market is defined as firms doing roughly $5 million to $100 million in sales annually. Throughout my career as a CEO, I have felt what can only be described as "limited power." In a sense, I have always been uncomfortable with this limited power, vacillating between a feeling of not having enough power and concern about properly using the *real* power that I did have. The responsibility of leadership can have that effect on you.

THE ELEMENTS OF GREAT LEADERSHIP

There are four elements to great leadership:

1. The ability to make good things happen that would not happen otherwise, i.e., to be creative and effective in the way goals are estab-

lished, communicated and pursued, and in the way opportunities and problems are addressed.

2. The ability to decide what to do, when it is not clear what to do.

3. The ability to quickly and equitably resolve conflicts between what we call the four nexus of contracts groups of a business: the employees, the vendors, the shareholders, and the customers.

4. The ability to perform the first three functions in a trust-building manner, i.e., ethically.

My purpose in writing about business ethics is to tell you what I have observed: there is real power, life-changing power, to ethical behavior in business. We are going to talk about what that power is and how that power is derived by those who behave in ways that are trust building. "Business ethics" is not an oxymoron!

THE FOUNDATION STATEMENT OF ETHICS

THE FOUNDATION STATEMENT OF ETHICS IS AS FOLLOWS:

Ethics deals with the gains and losses we experience as a result of our relationships with others.

THE PROBLEM OF SCALE

In our discussion of ethics, we are going to experience what scientists call the problem of scale. Scientists have observed that when you look at a lab sample in biology with the naked eye you see one thing. When you look at the same sample with a 10,000-power microscope you see something completely different, but it isn't any simpler. When you look at the sample with a 100,000-power microscope, again you see something completely different, and unfortunately again, it is no simpler. Business ethics has that same property to it. As we get into this material, you will see things that you didn't see before, but it is not going to make the issues related to business ethics any easier. However, you will have the roadmap for building trust!

THE ASSESSMENT QUESTIONS OF BUSINESS ETHICS

Business ethics is a complicated subject because it must deal with questions like the following:

- "What course of conduct or relationship, contractual or otherwise, gave rise to an expected gain?"

- "How did subsequent events differ from what was expected?"

- "Did the parties to the agreement expect the same outcomes?"

- "Did the parties to the agreement share their expectations with each other accurately and completely before relying on and allowing the other parties to rely upon the agreement?"

- "What losses occurred, and who *should* bear them? Why?"

These are called the assessment questions of business ethics.

CONTRACTS AND RELATED ISSUES

In business the course of conduct or the relationship that gives rise to an expected gain is often spelled out in a written contract. We will discuss several facets of contracts, such as behavior or courses of conduct that give rise to an expected gain, as with a marriage commitment. We will discuss problems related to our social contract. Rousseau's essay, "The Social Contract," dealt with issues related to the rights and obligations that people enjoy and are burdened by when they join a community — that is when they choose to live in a city or a town.

We will also discuss the rights and obligations that we have to people who are not parties to our contracts. This becomes an issue in the case of pollution, for example. When people pollute the air, not only do we have to clean our clothes more often, but also our health suffers; and to take pollution to its logical consequence, unchecked pollution will eventually destroy life on earth as we know it. These are not trivial examples, but ones used frequently to describe what economists call *externalities* — conditions that give rise to gains and losses among those who are not party to an agreement (i.e., parties who are "external" to any existing contract).

We will explore four principles of ethical power:

1. For a given level of capability, ethical behavior increases the number of people who will deal with you, and conversely.

2. Transaction costs are reduced as the level of trust increases.

3. Ethical behavior increases the motivation to succeed at task because it increases the value of the prize and the probability of success, while reducing the value of the loss and the probability of the loss.

4. Ethical behavior has an aesthetic quality to it. It is beautiful, and draws us to it and to those who exhibit it.

To the extent possible, we will attempt to quantify that power. Unfortunately, some of these concepts defy accounting, so we have to use our analytical and deductive reasoning, as well as our intuition, in order to fully feel the power. We will discuss trust-building and trust-eroding behavior, as a new twist on an old subject.

We will not discuss good people or bad people.

We will touch on the three principles of business ethics: the dismal principle, the heuristic principle, and the principle of remorse.

We will review in detail the five categories of trust-building behavior and then we'll discuss the four requirements of trust-building behavior. We will use the principles we develop here to answer the assessment questions as they apply to specific cases.

Let's begin.

1 Can You Tell a Lie?

Some time ago I gave a presentation on business ethics to a marketing class at the Graduate School of Business at the University of Cincinnati under the direction of Professor Chris Allen. It was an early Saturday morning class during finals week. Philosophy Professor Bob Faaborg, who also teaches business ethics, had joined us. Accordingly, I was very excited to present this material.

Jeff Berk was the first student to come to class. He had been up all night working on a marketing case. Jeff stumbled in and took a seat in the back row of the classroom. I walked back to introduce myself by offering a "good morning" greeting, my name and a handshake. Jeff responded coldly: "I'm Jeff Berk and this better be good!"

I thought to myself, "Jeff must be special!" so I asked, "What is your goal for this session, Jeff?"

Jeff replied without a smile or hesitation: "My goal is to stay awake."

I responded that that was my goal for him, as well. Once class began, I wanted to see if I could help Jeff achieve his goal by giving him a little adrenaline spike. So I asked him to stand and join me in the following mind experiment:

Imagine, Jeff, that I am interviewing you for a job and that there are only three remaining candidates for the job; you're one of the three. Imagine further that I ask you the following: "Can you tell a lie?"

The entire class had turned to face Jeff, who was clearly exhibiting some anxiety about the question and the pressure of having to answer before his classmates. He managed to say, "Yes." However, based on his body language and the nervousness in his voice, he was not totally pleased to have to answer in that way.

I responded with an additional question, "When would you?"

Jeff continued, "I would to serve a greater good."

I asked for an example, and received a Joycean stream of consciousness:

"My daughter will ask me why I do something a certain way, why she can or cannot do something, and she's not always capable of understanding the clear, true answer — the answer that comes closest to taking all points of consideration, so sometimes to simplify things and to help her get to the place where I honestly believe she needs to be, I may lie to preserve the greater good — to get the child to learn certain patterns, certain pieces of knowledge, and you can't incorporate that all at once, so sometimes they need something different they can build on!"

"That's a good answer," I said smiling, "That's a good answer under pressure." Jeff breathed a sigh of relief, and so did the class.

What was good about the answer was not only what he said, but also "how" he answered. Jeff responded as though he was concerned about answering truthfully. But he was also concerned about how we would perceive his integrity in light of the answer. This type of reaction is often reflective of someone who is sensitive about behaving ethically — a person from whom ethical behavior is a priority.

I then shared the following experience:

Years ago, I met a man named Kurt Einstein, who ran an executive search firm in New York. I attended a presentation he made on interviewing executives. Afterward, I told him that our firm was growing at an alarming rate and had a voracious appetite for good people at all levels, especially middle and senior management. I explained that I had a terrible batting average with new hires, and that I was especially concerned with making an assessment of the character of prospective employees.

He said, "Louie, I want you to write this script down. There are two questions that you must ask every candidate in order to begin an ethical assessment. Now write it down, because I don't want to use unnecessary words. Keep the script simple.

'Question 1: Can you tell a lie?

'Then remain silent. You just watch and wait for the response: 99% of the people you interview can tell a lie and are going to say, 'Yes, I can.' Pay attention to their

body language and speech pattern. Do they appear as someone who is concerned about answering truthfully?

'Then you must follow their response with the next question.

'Question 2: When would you?'"

"After that question, just wait. See what they have to say and watch how they answer the question, because the behavior, the delayed speech pattern or anxiety over the question, may be as important to you as the answer itself. These are very tough questions. It's not clear to the person being interviewed what the motivation of the question is. They may appear to be some sort of trick questions. But they're very serious questions. If you're asked a question in response, then firmly repeat: 'When would you tell a lie?' The inability to get a straight answer to the second question is a clear sign of trouble! However, you will be amazed at the kind of answers you'll get from different people."

Kurt was right. I have been amazed as I've used these questions throughout my career. I was interviewing a fellow for a CEO spot one time. This fellow looked sensational — both on paper and in person. (People always weigh the appearance of the candidate out of proportion with the other available evidence — that's one of the reasons there are so many good-looking, articulate, and incompetent people in business!) This candidate was also articulate, and had relevant experience. He said quickly, "Yes, I can tell a lie." He did so without any apparent concern for the question, which I always find disturbing. When someone experiences a little anxiety over their response, I feel it is trust-building. Maybe I feel that way because I squirmed the first time I heard and had to answer these questions.

I followed my script and I asked, "When would you?"

He quickly said, "I would tell a lie if it meant getting an order from a customer."

What do *you* think about that? In my mind, the interview was over with that answer because I wouldn't tell a lie to get an order. It took me about five minutes to end the interview.

I really didn't know how to respond to his answer. I was angry about it, however, because I had invested a lot of time and effort with this candidate, which clearly had been wasted. Now, I ask these questions early in the process.

Jeff Berk's answer was a solid answer under pressure, a trust-building answer. But probably the best answer I ever received came from a fellow who had been caught in a corporate downsizing. He was 55 years old and a solid candidate. (I should have hired him; I didn't. I hired a guy that bombed!)

I asked, "Can you tell a lie?"

"I can, I'm embarrassed to say. I can tell a lie," he lamented slowly, "but I hate to."

I asked, "When would you?"

He said, "Unfortunately in business, you are put into positions from time to time where people ask you questions, the answers of which — because of their interests and intentions — they are not entitled to, information which they could use to hurt you or which might trigger some kind of a reprisal from them if the information were disclosed."

I concur with his assessment but marveled at his ability to answer my questions so completely and briefly under the pressure of a job interview.

Generally, I have found that trust-building answers to these questions have to do with the "greater good," discharging your responsibility to protect a third party or even yourself from a loss, coupled with a visible anxiety over the questions and answers.

The example from Philosophy 101 is as follows: A man comes to your door with a shotgun, asks you if your father is home and tells you that he intends to kill him. The right answer is *not*, "Just a minute, please, I'll get him!"

Like everything else, these questions represent only a beginning. But if you have a clear difference on these issues in the interviewing process, proceed only with great caution!

THE WHITE LIE

I have an aunt who got the idea that I love a particular dish she serves from time to time. Unfortunately, I really don't care for it at all. However, she serves it to me frequently and with great pride, and always asks, "How is it?"

I respond with a white lie: "It's just like always."

She is pleased with this answer. I don't hurt her feelings, and if my response is a crime, then it's a victimless crime! Because of my feelings for her, I can't bring myself to answer with total candor.

CONFLICTS OF INTEREST

The serious cases in business ethics are not a matter of white lies, but conflicts of interest. Because we are continuously dealing with people whose interests are not the same as ours, we often face this condition in business.

INTUITION

Generally speaking, people who exhibit trust-building behavior over a long period of time have a rock-solid sense of what right and wrong is, built on an intuition about the gains and losses that people experience as a result of conflicts of interest which are inherent in their relationships with us and others.

Here's an interesting story in this connection. While on a flight to Los Angeles, I was working on a paper, and this bold young man (age 14) interrupted me. He introduced himself as Nick and asked me what I did. I told him. He said, "I'm going to be a CEO someday."

I asked, "Really?"

He said "Yeah."

I thought I'd test Nick's CEO mettle and have a little fun at the same time. I asked, "Nick, can you tell a lie?"

He said slowly and thoughtfully, "Yes, I can tell a lie."

I said, "When would you?"

He said, "I would tell a lie to keep a secret that a friend had shared with me."

I asked him, "Give me an example."

"Something that might be troubling someone," he said. "Like if he shared something, a secret, with me to get my opinion. Then the next day at school if someone asked, 'Hey, Nick, do you know about the secret?'"

I asked, "Would you tell a lie then?"

He said, "Yeah, I would tell a lie then."

I asked, "What would you tell them?"

Nick said, "I'd tell them I don't know."

It was a beautiful sequence, especially when you consider Nick's age. I concurred with Nick: "I don't know" might be the right response even though it was a lie — he did know.

Nick's interest was to avoid violating the confidence that his friend's secret represented so that his friend would not suffer a loss as a result of the disclosure of that secret. When Nick was questioned about the secret, the questioner's interest was in gaining or sharing information about the secret. Their interests were in conflict, i.e., not the same. Nick's response preserved the confidence. Nick's questioner was not entitled to know the truth.

Nick had shared with me a lesson that I believe is a hard lesson to learn: ethics is partly intuitive. I believe that you *might* be able to learn or improve upon your sense of right and wrong, especially if you're exposed to the right kind of people. But I believe that there is a certain intuition about right and wrong that you must have at the beginning. It is an aptitude type of thing: some people can run fast naturally, and with work, they'll run a little faster. I think it's a similar thing with ethics. Some people understand intuitively what these issues are. It is often hard to discuss them. It's often difficult to articulate what's right and wrong and why, especially, for example, when you're asked a series of questions by an older man you've never seen before. But Nick could and did answer my questions that evening very well. I'm always quite amazed at how well developed this ethical sense can be at a very young age.

More than 250 years ago, Immanuel Kant wrote *Critique of Pure Reason* which is concerned with what we can know. It wasn't too long before he turned to the subject of what we can know about ethical behavior. He was searching for a set of categorical imperatives, a set of rules, or at least one ethical rule that would have to be followed no matter what. He did so because he was concerned that people do lie, and that we can all imagine cases where the right thing to do is to tell a lie, as we've already established.

THE ETHICAL DILEMMA

What can we say about ethics in a business world where 99% of us can and do tell lies, and where there are conditions which the right thing to do *is* to tell a lie?

In the case of business theory, there is a lack of conceptual framework about which to discuss business. It is the combination of this lack of a conceptual framework and the fact that business people can and do tell lies that dampens the enthusiasm of business people for a discussion of ethics.

My enthusiasm for solutions to the ethical problems of business has not been dampened at all, however. As a business leader, I've spent a lifetime dealing with ethical problems. Every day, I am dealt a steady stream of situations which represent potential ethical *dilemmas* that can't be avoided and if untreated or not treated early, will often mature with the passage of time into ever more serious ethical *problems*. I have developed approaches to these problems because I have had to deal with these problems. And still do. I have no choice. I have to make good decisions as a CEO that not only allow me to continue to be gainfully employed, but that I feel good about intuitively and that make it possible for me to sleep at night — that is the challenge!

Fortunately, it is the exception to find yourself in a situation where telling a lie is the right thing to do. But from a logical point of view, one exception destroys the rule. That fact is what Kant and others have grappled with throughout the ages.

2 Why Business Ethics Is A Forgiving Condition

The good news is that business ethics is the most forgiving condition possible in the discussion of ethics. Imagine that the universe of ethical problems is represented by a circle three feet in diameter. Business ethics must necessarily represent a smaller universe. It's smaller because it's a special condition. Maybe it's two feet in diameter, because we are omitting larger questions that are dealt with in ethics, but not in business ethics.

For example, we're not going to discuss whether we should be in business or not. We're not going to discuss whether we should be in a specific business. We are here to discuss *behavior, given that we're in business.* Professors of philosophy have to deal with questions of whether or not there should be businesses at all. We're not going to deal with that. Philosophers, politicians, parents, and many others are concerned about whether people should be in the tobacco business. I'm not, at least for the purpose of this book! I'm here to discuss business ethics given that you're *in business,* regardless of the business you're in. Once we get our arms around the narrower questions, then we can move to the larger, loftier, more difficult — and really more important — broader questions of ethics. But that will be beyond the scope of this book.

ETHICS AND THE BUSINESS LEADER

As I point out to MBA students: your destiny is a leadership position in business. Very few MBA students will go into business, be assimilated into a company, and work on a technical track all alone. That doesn't happen often. It can happen, but most MBA students are going into business to deal with and manage other humans, and that will put them into an ethical crucible.

But from an ethics point of view, business ethics is the most forgiving condition, for the following two reasons: first, we're going to ignore the question of whether there should be businesses or whether we should be in business or not.

And second, and most importantly, the existence of contracts.

Figure 2-1
**THE NEXUS OF CONTRACTS: The Flow
of Consideration and Competitive Offers**

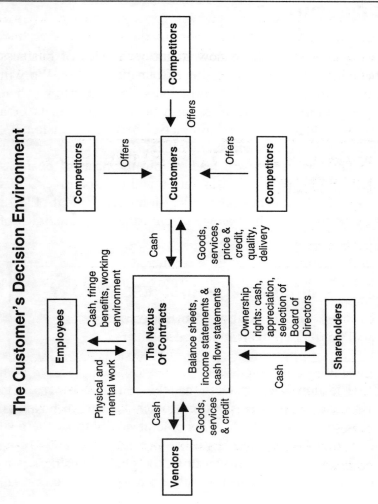

THE CONFLICT OF INTEREST PRINCIPLE

Let's make a transition now to the principles of business theory. This is the foundation of our discussion. We will move from these five principles into a flow chart representation of a business as a nexus of contracts or a coming together of contracts between customers, employees, vendors and shareholders.

This discussion will lead us into the heart of business ethics. The flow of Consideration and Competitive Offers (Figure 2-1) is the customer's decision environment. Please refer to the flow chart as we discuss the five principles of business theory:

PRINCIPLE 1 OF BUSINESS THEORY

**The goal of business is
to have a customer.**

The flow chart reflects that the goal of business is to have customers, because no customers means no business. It's as simple as that. Now, people normally think the goal of business is to make a profit. It's not. That is not an operational concept. If you think the goal of business is to make a profit, you will not only go down the wrong road, you will not be able to explain the existence of non-profit organizations.

Profit is covered in the second principle of business.

PRINCIPLE 2 OF BUSINESS THEORY

Profit is a requirement of a business.

If you're making losses, your business is not going to survive, unless the losses can be turned to profits. (How much time you have to do this is a key element of the subject of business strategy.) Profits are required so that sufficient cash is available to flow as consideration between all of the contracts in the nexus of contracts — contracts that give rise to a business. A business cannot indefinitely meet the contractual obligations of the employees, the vendors, the customers, or the shareholders if it's making losses. Even non-profit organizations need a "profit" in order to survive, although their income statements use different words.

PRINCIPLE 3 OF BUSINESS THEORY

A business is a nexus of contracts.

A business is a coming together of contracts between the customers, employees, vendors, and shareholders. We are going to talk about these contracts shortly.

> ## PRINCIPLE 4 OF BUSINESS THEORY
>
> ### The competitors are out to take your customers away.

You can see on the flow chart that the customers are continuously being bombarded with competitive offers. If there's one thing that should be foremost in a CEO's mind, it is the existence of the ever-improving competitive offers that customers are constantly receiving — i.e., the course and speed of the competition. Designing offerings that represent more for less than the competition, delivering quality work on time while still making a profit, is the challenge of business.

> ## PRINCIPLE 5 OF BUSINESS THEORY
>
> ### We are all selling personal services.

Everybody in business is selling a personal service. Business is a human thing. We're each selling human services to other humans as individuals, or as individuals who are representatives of other groups of individuals — e.g., employees and shareholders.

Every business is the brainchild of an entrepreneur, maybe with the help of a friend or two. Generally, a business gets started in a garage, a basement or a kitchen. For Henry Ford, it was a garage; for Microsoft's Bill Gates, it was a kitchen table; for Amway's Rich DeVos and Jay Van Andel, it was a basement. What did they have at the beginning? They had an idea, they had their physical and mental work capacity and a place to mess around, and that's it. That's one of the reasons why a start-up business is so difficult to get off the ground. There is so little in place to build on. But once the business takes off, entrepreneurs — normally the main shareholders — realize their power is limited. They can't do everything alone. Consider Mary Kay: once she found customers for her cosmetics, her business grew, and she had to hire some employees. She also needed additional vendors to make the cosmetics and supply other goods and services. As her business grew further, she needed additional shareholders. From Mary Kay's initial idea, you see that this nexus of contracts — this coming together of contracts — makes it possible for the entrepreneur to keep ever more competitive offers flowing to the customers and back them up by an ever greater capacity to deliver because of the power of additional vendors, employees, and shareholders.

THE FLOW OF CASH

Notice on the flow chart in Figure 2-1, the flow of consideration indicated by the arrows that run to and from the members of the four nexus of contract groups. For the employees, they are sharing their physical and mental work for cash, fringe benefits, and all the intangibles that go with the employment package, including the quality of the work environment.

For the vendors, they are exchanging goods and services on credit for cash, normally to be paid thirty days hence or at some earlier or later date.

The customers are exchanging cash for goods and services. The customers are vitally concerned about the price, quality, and delivery of the offering relative to the competitive offers that are available.

And, of course, the shareholders are interested in ownership rights. Shareholders are willing to exchange their cash now for the ownership rights they hope will be converted into a stream of cash or a lump sum cash payment at some future point in time. Whether it's dividends or long-term capital gains, shareholders are looking for a cash flow at a later date in exchange for an investment made now.

You'll notice in Figure 2-1 that at the center of each of these contracts is cash. Cash makes the world go around. Without profits, however, there is no cash to maintain a stable nexus of contracts unless the shareholders are willing to let a business "burn cash" with losses and willing to invest more cash into the business to replenish what has been burned.   Businesses that are growing often find themselves in a tight cash position even if they are profitable.

One of the reasons that growth is hell is because you have to pay employees and vendors for goods and services before you can deliver and get paid for the goods and services provided to or delivered to your customers. In other words, cash outlays to your employees and vendors normally come before you can collect your money from your customers!

In order to be able to raise enough cash from banks and shareholders to finance a growing business, you must accurately predict future cash disbursements to vendors and employees, as well as sales and the ultimate collection of cash from your customers.   The problem of accurately predicting the future cash flows is the reason that financing a growing operation is difficult.

Accordingly, if there was ever a group that had to behave in a trust-building manner it is people in business finance.   Because banks and shareholders are relying on these forecasts of the future, forecasts have to be presented that will be realized, or else confidence and trust in the management will be eroded.   When you continually miss your forecasts, people conclude you either lack capability or integrity, and neither of those conditions can be read charitably.

THE CONFLICT OF INTEREST PRINCIPLE

What every entrepreneur discovers quickly is that their limited power drives them into agreements with other people. When we say agreements, we mean contracts with other people. A contract, of course, is a delicate balance of rights and obligations between people whose interests do not coincide. But from an ethics point of view, business ethics is the most forgiving condition in ethics, because as consenting adults selling personal services, the contract defines to some extent what our rights and obligations are, including our ability to represent our company in agreements with others.

Unfortunately, one of the stickiest areas in business ethics is the relationship an employer has with his/her employees, because of all the contracts in the nexus, the employee agreement is typically the most poorly defined and normally covers the longest period of time. When you enter a business, you almost always end up working for someone who didn't interview you. Later on, as you get promoted or transferred, you find yourself dealing with people that weren't there at the beginning of your entire career, people who could not have outlined the "what" and "how" of your career even if they had been there at your hire date.

However, even in the most perfect agreement, whether it be a marriage, an unemployment contract, a purchase order, or a long-term vendor relationship, we can all imagine receiving a little more in the way of rights and a little less in the way of obligations.

Here's a little story to illustrate the point:

For three generations in our family there has been a rule about sharing dessert, which says that whoever cuts must let the other choose. One day I was watching the Reds game with my sons, Nicholas, Peter and Paul, who were about 12, 7, and 5 years old, respectively; my wife Pam was out. There was half of a cherry pie left for dessert. We made our sandwiches and there was the pie. We all spied it. We ate our sandwiches quickly while we watched the game. Peter and Paul jumped up after lunch to get their pie. All of a sudden there was a big argument. I couldn't make out what they were saying, but the decibel level was rising. This was usually bad for Paul, the younger brother. I ran in and said, "Hey, what's going on, guys?" As it turns out, Nicholas had gone into the kitchen and eaten two-thirds of the remaining pie. There was one piece of pie left, and Peter and Paul both wanted it.

I said, "Guys, you know the rules. In the Strike house whoever cuts has to let the other one choose!"

Peter, the oldest one, said, "Well, Dad, that's the problem."

"What's the problem?"

Paul offered, "Peter wants me to cut because he knows I'm the little brother and I can't cut it straight, so he's going to get the big piece."

There was a faint smile creeping into the corner of Peter's mouth. I knew that Paul was telling the truth.

I said, "Peter, that is so disappointing. What kind of leadership are you showing to your little brother?"

Peter said, "Okay, Dad. I wanted Paul to cut, but I'm only 7, and I can't cut it that good either, and Paul wants the bigger piece."

So I got angry and ate the pie. And that question has never come up since.

Peter came in later and said, "That's never going to happen again."

I asked, "Why not Peter?"

Peter said, "We should have known that if we got into a fight you'd eat the pie and then both of us would lose out on our dessert."

That's a good story to keep in mind as a memory aid, because even in the most perfect relationship, like two brothers who are best friends, we can always imagine getting a little bit more and giving a little bit less as we negotiate an agreement.

All the nexus of contracts groups in business experience this conflict.

As a result, a priority for great business leadership is to manage these relationships in a stable manner *and* in an ever-growing manner, so that you can improve your offering to the customer, as well as to offer your employees a richer working experience and better compensation; offer your vendors larger orders, and finally, offer your shareholders a better rate of return at a lower level of risk. To do this successfully, the needs of each group must be met, or people will defect from your nexus of contracts group.

We don't want people of character and capability waltzing out of our environment. We need the best possible people in all of our nexus of contracts groups. We don't want the vendors, employees, customers, or shareholders to lose confidence in us or to believe that their needs can be met better by competitive offers, or that they will suffer a loss dealing with us. If it's a public company, it's easy for shareholders to sell their shares, but if enough do, the value of the firm will decline precipitously. In the case of key employees, if they are not treated fairly, good people will leave. They can leave your department, or your company, because they will have better offers. Good people will eventually have offers.

Often, by the time management consultants go into a turnaround situation, many of the good people have already left.

THE STAGES OF NEGOTIATION

There are three stages of negotiation: (1) discovery; (2) discussion; and (3) performance. Each stage reveals aspects of character and capability. Your reputation and ethical stance will affect how the three stages play out.

Stage one is a period of discovery of indefinite length. In the business community, your reputation determines who is going to deal with you. If you deal in a manner that erodes trust, then people are going to know it. The smaller the community, the greater the likelihood that everyone is going to know it. Cincinnati is a relatively small community when compared to Chicago. The New York metropolitan area is larger still. But even in New York City, your reputation will get around, because even when we are swimming in a large pond, we only swim in a portion of the pond or in certain channels of the pond, and under these circumstances, what goes around comes around.

Figure 2-2

THE STAGES OF NEGOTIATION

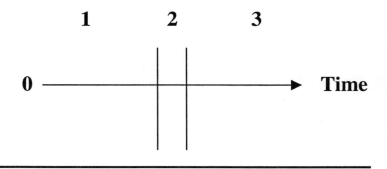

The World's Greatest Car Salesman & the Rule of 250

Joe Gerard is reputed to be the world's greatest car salesman. He worked in Detroit. One of his marketing techniques was to go to a football game and just throw his business cards out over the stands at half time. It was an obnoxious, direct marketing technique, but he didn't care. He sold a lot of cars. Using this technique was successful because selling is a numbers game, and at every game some people would pick these cards up and put them in their pockets. Over time, Joe received their calls, people liked the way they were treated, and the rest is history.

He also used to go to weddings and funerals and copy down the names of people attending. He'd return to his office, look up the addresses and put these people on his mailing list. Joe was not merely bold, he was smart. He noticed that the average number of people invited to a wedding or a funeral is 250 people.

So he came up with his "Rule of 250":

THE RULE OF 250:

If you can do something nice for someone, you could affect your reputation by up to 250 people. Conversely, if you do something to hurt someone — something that is unfair — you could put a message out to 250 people in the community that you are not trustworthy.

Joe imagined "250" on everybody's forehead as a memory aid to remind him to be nice to everyone. So although he had obnoxious selling techniques, those who called Joe found that he was a good man to deal with. He had a lot of repeat business. If you could get over the shock

of his introductory techniques, you might give him a try —
a lot of people did, and with good results.

Putting Reputation Through a Time Test

Because the discovery stage can be long, your reputation
will be on display for a long time. This can be an asset, if
your reputation can stand up under the test of time.

In the early 1980's, I was president of Hess &
Eisenhardt.   We built specialty automobiles, including
funeral coaches, limousines, convertibles, and armored cars
for heads of state. We presented a proposal to Jaguar of
North America to take the XJS coupe and make 3,000 units
per year into convertibles.   Hess & Eisenhardt was a
hundred-year-old company with a solid reputation in the
automotive world as a coach builder of capability and
integrity. At any point in time, we thought we were only
one or two months away from a significant production
contract. And we finally did get it.

Originally, we got the appointment because of our
capability reputation — because of the work we had done
with General Motors on funeral coaches and limousines,
and with the Secret Service on armored cars. Part of the
reason we got the order, however, was that we were so
persistent in our calling efforts. Jaguar knew that we had a
good management team. But they also found out that we
could stick with the marketing effort for six years,
including a six-year stream of ever more compelling
proposals, after being faced with a new set of obstacles

month after month. Maybe we just weren't that smart, but the way we conducted ourselves over a long period of time gave Jaguar added confidence to deal with us. This is the prologue to the first principle of ethical power.

THE FIRST PRINCIPLE OF ETHICAL POWER

THE FIRST PRINCIPLE OF ETHICAL POWER

For a given level of capability, ethical behavior increases the number of people who will deal with you, and conversely.

(Because integrity and capability operate jointly, we will only deal with people who have sufficient capability for the task at hand. More on this shortly.)

This is not a trivial source of power. People who are capable but that behave in a trust-eroding manner often can't understand why their careers are going badly. They can't understand, because people normally aren't going to tell you that they are disappointed in the way you treated them. You normally can't get that feedback. If you don't do what you say you are going to do, you often won't get

another chance, even if you're capable. Through the power
of the Rule of 250, your trust-eroding behavior with one
person can affect up to 250 others. That is how a
marketplace becomes contaminated with a bad reputation.

We often say: you can't make a good deal with bad
people. You can't make a good deal with people who
behave in a trust-eroding manner. But just as trust-eroding
behavior will create a bad reputation, trust-building
behavior over time will create a good reputation. Keep in
mind, though, that bad news always travels farther and
faster, and is weighted more heavily than good news. One
debacle can destroy a lifetime of good work.

THE RADIUS OF TRUST

It is as if every organization and every human being has a
radius of trust. People who have had long careers and have
managed to equitably balance the interests of the people
they've dealt with can enjoy a large radius of trust. For
others it is smaller. People who would tell you a lie even if
the truth sounded better often never understand why their
radius of trust is about as big as the head of a pin and they
can't find people with whom to enter into any significant
agreements. The radius of trust is a very powerful thing.

Character and Capability

If you come up with the cure for cancer and are unethical, people are still going to deal with you. Some people will deal with the devil to gain the magic they seek.

Generally, however, reputation is based on both capability and integrity, working together. We assess the integrity *and* capability of our associates before we enter into an agreement, because we wish to enjoy the benefits, the rights, that our contract is going to provide to us. If we think people don't have the capability to deliver, or they won't deliver because of a lack of integrity, or they will try to change the deal at the end or at some point in the future, then we are reluctant to enter into any agreement at all, even a test order. Here's the principle again: ethical behavior increases the number of people who will deal with you, and conversely.

The *conversely* is critical.

Watch the Revolving Door

In the business community, people are sensitive to any changes in a nexus of contracts of a business, especially with vendors and our key employees. When you see a firm that has a revolving door of employees, including senior management, something is wrong. Remember that the good people can leave — they will get offers. Sometimes they leave even in a year when there are record earnings.

Baldwin-United Corporation, for example, went bankrupt in the early 80's. It was a Cincinnati firm, and a darling of Wall Street that grew large through a series of acquisitions. It was tremendous success story. But something unusual happened. Tim Hartman, the chief financial officer at that time, announced that he was taking a job as a CFO for another company. When I heard the news, I thought that it didn't make sense. Baldwin-United was a great company. Tim, who I knew personally, albeit not well, was certainly in the inner circle of the top four or five people. He had stock options, was well compensated, lived in a nice city, and yet, he left? Why? There was just a little paragraph about it in the local papers, but there was a good deal of discussion about it in the business community. In less than eighteen months, Baldwin was in bankruptcy.

Maybe there is no connection to Tim's departure and the subsequent financial demise of Baldwin-United. Maybe there is nothing to Tim Hartman's story, other than that another opportunity came up — an opportunity too good to pass up. But maybe Tim saw something in the situation that made it or might make it unstable, even though the firm was showing record profits and its stock price was at an all-time high. Could he have seen a hint of their demise? I don't know, but as a CFO, he certainly was in a position to do so. He was responsible for putting together financial forecasts for the company.

In any event, people are very sensitive when vendors, employees, and key customers "leave a business" — drop out of the nexus of contracts. News like this gets around a community, because it can be bad news, especially when there is a pattern of multiple defections.

The thing to keep in mind is that in the negotiation process, stage one can be a long period of discovery, during which time what you are by reputation, as well as recent developments within your nexus of contracts group, will determine who is going to deal with you and how.

3

Negotiation and Ethical Power

S tage two of negotiation is usually a brief period in which the rights and obligations of the proposed contract are discussed and agreed to. For an employee, it's an interviewing process. For a vendor relationship, it might be the discussion of a purchase order or a long-term production agreement. For a new shareholder, it could be some kind of a discovery and analysis process, and of course, for customers, it is the sale. Although we spent six years in a stage one to persuade Jaguar cars, it took us a fraction of that time to get down to a real contract to build convertibles once there was a meeting of the minds.

Because the second stage is short, it's also very stressful, especially if you are contemplating an exchange transaction where you are buying or selling something. After the closing, all the performance required by the contract has been completed — as in the sale of a piece of real estate, a business, a product line, a division, or some asset. It's a stressful condition, because if the people you are dealing with have misrepresented a material fact, you might not have any recourse against them, unless in the agreement there are representations and warranties that will survive the closing on some basis. Even then, you might be faced with the costs, aggravation, potential counterclaims, and uncertainty of litigation. Unfortunately, by the time court relief is obtained, the other party might not be able to make us whole for the loss we experienced at their hands, nor are they able to return us to our original position. As a result, it is in the second phase of a negotiation that we observe the second source of ethical power.

THE SECOND PRINCIPLE OF ETHICAL POWER

> ## THE SECOND PRINCIPLE OF ETHICAL POWER
>
> **Transaction costs are reduced as the level of trust increases.**

Transaction costs are the costs that you must incur in order to feel comfortable enough to enter into an agreement at all — for example, the amount of due diligence and related work that you, your accountants, and attorneys have to do in terms of the structure of the deal, and the assessment of the capability, and the integrity of the other party.

The Power of Credible Customers

The existence of transactions costs is one of the reasons that the customers with whom you deal are so important to a prospective customer. In a sense, who your current customers are is the number-one thing in selling to a prospective customer, especially if you are in a business that sells business to business. When I was president of Hess & Eisenhardt and potential customers wanted to know who our existing customers were, we could say the State Department, the Secret Service, Cadillac Motor Division of General Motors and their related dealers, the Ford Motor Company, and Jaguar Cars. These are solid customers with high requirements for any vendor. So any firm that was looking to deal with us knew we had already passed a substantial battery of tests in order to qualify as a vendor to some of the most difficult and demanding customers in the world. These tests were subsequently backed up by the delivery of quality — reliable products delivered on time at market prices over long periods of time.

The legal and accounting fees you must incur as part of the due diligence and the agreement development process can be high in order to protect yourself. Therefore, you have to be sensitive to the reputation and, subsequently, the course of conduct of the people you are dealing with before and during the negotiation process. If when you sit across from the other party you can tell your legal counsel that you don't need an airtight agreement — both belts and suspenders, if you will — because you are dealing with good people, then transaction costs go down and the calendar time to make the deal is reduced. Accordingly, the probability of making a deal increases. In addition, if you have to be tough in drafting an agreement, you erode some of the trust between the parties. If you become unwilling to grant as many benefits to the other party because of a lack of trust, you may be withholding the benefits that the other side may need to carry an agreement through to closure, i.e., your chances of closing the deal at all are reduced.

Long-Term, Value-Creating Agreements

The closing is just the beginning of the third or performance stage of this negotiation.

The most interesting agreements in business are not exchange agreements where the closing represents the end of the process. Instead, they are agreements where the closing is just the beginning. For example, someone accepts your proposal for employment with your firm. It is at the point when your proposal is accepted that you enter the performance phase. The agreement is just the beginning of what could be a 40-year career. When you agree to build a plant to build limousines in Detroit, or you agree to completely refurbish your plant in Cincinnati in order to build

Jaguar convertibles for Jaguar Cars, then closing the agreement is the beginning.

The most interesting agreements in business depend on leadership being able to attract people who are willing to enter into long-term, value-creating agreements that will be stable over time. These agreements depend on each party's assessment of the character and capability of the other party, and the prediction that the hoped for benefits of the agreement for both parties will be realized.

TRUST-BUILDING

Francis Fukuyama wrote a book called *Trust, The Social Virtues and Creation of Prosperity*. Fukuyama argues that trust in a society determines what that society is capable of. He says the United States, Germany, and Japan are the high-trust societies of the world. Cooperation requires trust. It takes a high degree of cooperation to build a great industrial company. It takes many cooperating companies to establish a great industrial economy — an economy capable of taking on monumental tasks like going to war or putting a man on the moon. It may be no coincidence then that the high-trust societies in the world were responsible for the beginning and the end of World War II.

Fukuyama contrasts high-trust societies with low-trust societies, China being an example of a low-trust society. In China, trust rarely extends beyond the immediate family. The same thing is true in Southern Italy. As a result, business enterprises in lower trust societies are small, because the key positions have to be staffed by family members.

You can't easily recruit large numbers of people into your family. As a result, businesses that must be carefully managed by immediate members of the family are necessarily small businesses.

When you look at the differences between Germany, which is a high-trust society, and France, which has a lower level of trust, one of the differences Fukuyama points out is the amount of supervision needed in factories. Where workers can be trusted to stick to their tasks and do high-quality work, less supervision is needed. This is not just of academic interest. According to Fukuyama, a factory supervisor in Germany can manage twenty-five employees on average, whereas in France, they manage sixteen. France does not have more supervisors on average than Germany because of a difference in organizational theory. They have them because they need them to get high-quality work done as cost-effectively as possible. The French and the Germans have experimented with more supervision and less supervision and they have found that it doesn't work as well. But Fukuyama argues French companies and, hence, the French economy experiences a penalty because of the difference in the level of trust, and therefore, supervision.

If Fukuyama is correct, we can crudely estimate Fukuyama's trust penalty by making some assumptions as shown in the table.

	Workers/ Supervisor	Supervisor/ 100 Workers	
1. France	16	6.25	
2. Germany	25	4.00	
3. Supervision cost per 100 workers:	**Labor**	**Supervision @ $25,000/each**	**Total**
a. France @ $20,000/yr/worker	$2,000,000	$156,250	$2,156,250
b. Germany @ $20,000/yr/worker	2,000,000	100,000	2,100,000
c. (3a − 3b)			56,250
d. (3c ÷ 3b)			2.7%
4. Manufacturing labor force @ 20% of the work force of 36,000,000 or 60% of France's assumed population of 60,000,000	7,200,000 workers		
5. Cost penalty of France relative to Germany per 100 workers per 3.c. above	$56,250/100 workers		
6. Cost penalty in $ (multiply 4 x 5)	$4.05 billion/year		
7. Investment required to create a job	$100,000		
8. Extra jobs created in Germany over France/year (6 ÷ 7)	40,000 jobs/year		

In the assumptions in the table, a worker is paid $20,000 a year in both France and Germany and supervisors are paid $25,000 a year.

Accordingly, every firm of 100 workers yields a penalty in additional supervision that the French must bear relative to the Germans. For a factory labor budget of $2 million a year the French firm will have $56,250 or 2.7 percent higher costs. Market pressures will require that this 2.7 percent cost difference be reflected in pricing decisions in a manner that results in a combination of somewhat higher prices or lower profits. We are going to ignore the joint effect of the pricing, profit and resultant lower volume penalties in this example, although the logical consequences of these penalties will be an additional burden on the French in free markets or markets where French goods and German goods are treated equally in terms of duties and tariffs.

Let's continue with our example and consider the implications for France and Germany in terms of job creation. Assuming that France has a population of about 60 million, a labor force of 60 percent of the population and a manufacturing labor force at about 20 percent of the labor force, then we find that the cost penalty in the French economy is about $4.05 billion a year. If you assume that it takes $100,000 investment to create a job, you'll see that the incremental supervision penalty of $4.05 billion a year results in an incremental job creation in the German economy of 40,000 jobs per year over the French economy on a population base of 60 million Germans. By stating the penalty for the French relative to the Germans on the basis of an equivalent population of 60 million, we can ignore the job creation on the German population in excess of 60 million.

Even if our assumptions are not quite accurate, we have been able to crudely shape Fukuyama's trust advantage of Germany versus France at least in the case of factory supervision. Every year that penalty is real, because politically, economically, and from a meaning-of-life point of view, job creation is vital. Given the same population base, when you have one economy that can create roughly 40,000 jobs a year more than a neighboring economy, then the magic of the continuous compounding of that advantage over a 10, 25, or 50-year period is significant! This is ignoring the effect of a market price penalty as just noted, which carries its own set of additional penalties that a less trusting economy must bear.

Let's make a transition to the Third Principle of Ethical Power.

4 Ethical Power and Human Motivation

How ethical behavior improves human motivation is the subject of this section. Intuitively, we know that the lack of integrity is demotivating. It saps our energy. In the case of a job or a career, when we are in an environment that lacks integrity, we are constantly agitated. We are always looking over our shoulder because we don't trust our supervisors or associates. Under these conditions, we expend tremendous physical and mental energy in order to cover our tracks, so that if something bad happens, we aren't going to lose our raise, promotion or job. We don't want to be blamed for anything. Not only are we trying to cover our backside, but we are actually limiting what we are trying to do.

What is going on to create these feelings?

THE BASIC QUESTIONS OF MOTIVATION

The questions of human motivation are as follows for any task *(t)*:

- How hard will we try?

- How long will we strive to succeed?

As with issues related to character and capability, the elements of motivation operate jointly, as well.

ATKINSON'S THEORY

On the surface, there are three elements motivating one to succeed at a task:

1. Our prediction of the likelihood of success, which we will denote as $P(s)$.

2. The value of the prize, which we will denote as $V(p)$.

3. Desire, an individual's innate motivation to achieve; that ability to try hard, which we all possess to a greater or lesser degree, which we will denote as $D(i)$.

In 1966, John W. Atkinson wrote *A Theory of Achievement Motivation*, which described the relationship of these three elements based on his work and the prior empirical studies that had been done on motivation. By that time, motivation had come to be called *achievement motivation*, i.e., the motivation to achieve.

Atkinson wanted to put forward a more comprehensive theory about human motivation than those existing at the time — if not a totally new theory, then at least a more complete and improved one. He succeeded.

The following are the key elements of Atkinson's theory:

Let the motivation that an individual displays toward task (t) be denoted as M(t). The formulation of the theory can be written as follows:

$$M(t) = D(i) \times V(p) \times P(s) \quad \text{(the gain term), where}$$

M(t) is the strength of the motivation (M) to achieve at task (t).

D(i) is the innate desire (d) of the individual (i). (I view this as a constant for each individual but varies between individual to individual; it does not vary with the task or over time.)

V(p) is the value (V) of the prize (p), i.e., the value of successfully completing the task (t) for individual (i).

*P(s) is the subjective probability (P) of success (s) for the
individual; in other words, the individual's perception of the
likelihood of success at task (t).*

When I first read Atkinson on this, I could see the
power of the formula immediately, and I got terribly excited. He had taken a nebulous, and yet terribly important,
concept and had expressed it in terms of discrete, operational components. I was armed with a concept I could understand and use every day in my business and personal life
to bring abut change. Whether or not the function is a simple multiplication equation, a higher order expression, a
logarithmic function or something else is not important.
What is important is that $M(t)$ varies directly with each of
the three variables.

Let's discuss each element.

Motivation to Achieve At Task (t): M(t)

The motivation *(M)* to achieve at task *(t)* for individual *(i)*,
written *M(t)*, is a function of the task. For example, my
sons are not as equally motivated to take out the garbage as
they are to join a pick-up game of basketball. They can be
too tired to move on garbage night but will enjoy an energy
spike when a friend calls to announce, "There's a pick-up
game at 10:00 p.m. in Burd's driveway and all the guys will
be there." Opportunity renews energy. Just how that re-
newal takes place is the subject of this discussion. However, in terms of my sons' energy system, I learned early on:

garbage "no" — basketball "yes." All tasks or opportunities are not created equal.

From a personal point of view, this points out the importance of pursuing one of possibly several careers that will be right for you. If you go to work where the tasks to be performed are the equivalent of "garbage" to you, then you and your employer will be disappointed. You will fail or, what is worse, be mediocre, and possibly spend your whole life doing something that you don't enjoy and aren't that good at.

What you can do and what you like to do are positively correlated for most of us over our careers.

Let's consider $D(i)$, the innate desire of the individual.

Individual Desire: D(i)

To simplify the analysis, Atkinson made the assumption that for each individual, $D(i)$ was equal to 1. He did this so that he could focus in on the impact of $V(p)$ and $P(s)$ and $M(t)$, which he regarded as the key elements.   However, as business leaders, we know that desire is not the same for each individual, so I have added the $D(i)$ term for our purposes.

Unfortunately, in the real world, the assessment of $D(i)$ is a serious issue. It is important that you assess your own $D(i)$, as well as develop some capability to make the assessment of the $D(i)$ of others. $D(i)$ relates to the ability to try hard even when the value of the prize is low. In part, it's a matter of one's energy level and work ethic. Some people work hard at whatever they are doing. Others do the bare minimum to get by on certain tasks. Some are excited about everything; others nothing. When we say, "Boy, he is really motivated," this is equivalent to saying that "he has a high $D(i)$ — he is not only motivated to do well at just high value tasks, but at every or almost every task."

It is as if the high $D(i)$'s have a V-8 engine in their chest running wide open on all projects. We all know people like this. Once you begin to consider differences in the $D(i)$'s of others, you will see the importance of being associated with others who enjoy approximately the same values and the same energy level and $D(i)$ that you do — the same or higher! This is true of your professional relationships and personal ones, as well. Agreement on an issue, such as how clean your house should be is a function of having not only the same values, but also a close match in $D(i)$.

When you are responsible to hire someone to fill a position and you have to select the best candidate from among five available candidates, your familiarity with the issues related to $D(i)$ is important. You should be looking for clues as to the level of each candidate's $D(i)$. You must be prepared to ask questions during the interview process that shed some light on the $D(i)$, answers that will impact the prediction as to who will make the biggest contribution to the department or company. (For example, "How do you spend your free time?" "What are your hobbies?" "What time do you go to bed and get up in the morning?")

Value of the Prize: V(p)

This brings us to the value of the prize, *V(p)*. Naturally, the prizes that are easiest to evaluate are those that carry a price tag or can be monetized on some basis — a new job, car or home. Consider the contrast in the value of a home to the value of a well-matched spouse or a child. The value of your loved ones cannot be quantified. Fortunately, in the case of a spouse or a child, we don't need to quantify these items to know the values are great. The key is to think through the *V(p)* for a task or process before or as you commit to it. Keep in mind that the value to us of that new home is our subjective value, or the utility value, of the home, not the price tag of $100,000. Similarly, the value of winning $1 million in the lottery is not the $1 million but the value or utility to you personally of having $1 million which, naturally, would be different if you were a millionaire, as opposed to a self-supporting college student.

When contemplating the *V(p)* keep in mind: as we accumulate gains, the incremental gains mean less to us than earlier gains.

Probability of Success: P(s)

Let's move now to the subjective probability of success at completing the task or achieving our goal, *P(s)*.

When you read Atkinson on this point, you find that researchers at the time related the *V(p)* to *P(s)* in this way:

The lower the probability of success, the higher the value of the prize. This is often the situation, i.e., we often want those things that are most difficult to get. However, in the real world, we don't need to make this kind of simplifying assumption in every case and, in fact, we can't always make this assumption, because "the best things in life are free."

Unfortunately, the $V(p)$ cannot often be quantified, and the subjective probability of success $P(s)$, although available to us is often substantially overstated, especially in cases where we have not experienced the same set of circumstances as before, which in the real world is much of the time. The $P(s)$ is often extraordinarily unstable over time, being especially sensitive to our most recent progress or disappointment.

This brings us to a restatement of the formula, because of the existence of loss potentials that some tasks necessarily involve.

Value of the Loss: V(l)

We've touched upon some of the problems with each of the elements of the equation. However, this formula has specifically ignored the fact that often the failure at the task (t) carries some penalty to it — and some loss. We know from decision theory that good decisions represent some gain, or at least the minimization of a loss, and that bad decisions cost us a gain at best and often carry with them a real loss.

How do we account for the loss potential in the theory of motivation?

)

Under circumstances where the task in question is such that the failure to succeed will result in a real loss, then the existence of that loss potential introduces an element of stress into the situation which serves to demotivate us. By that I mean that loss potentials not only dampen our motivation, but can also turn our motivation negative altogether, which means giving us a motivation to do nothing or, in some cases, gives us the motivation to pursue the opposite task, if such a task exists.

We can adjust our formula by merely adding to the gain term the negative value of a loss term, defined as follows:

$$D(i) \times V(l) \times P(l) \text{ (the loss term)}$$

where the following definitions are employed:

1. $D(i)$ is the innate desire *(d)* of the individual *(i)*, as defined above.

2. $V(l)$ is the value *(v)* of the loss *(l)*; the negative value of failing at task *(t)* for individual *(i)*.

3. $P(l)$ is the subjective probability *(p)* of loss *(l)* for the individual; in other words, the perception of the likelihood of failure which is also unstable and sensitive to our most recent experience. (Naturally, $P(l) + P(s) = 1.0$.)

We can now rewrite the formula, incorporating the gain term and the loss term as follows:

$$M(t) = \text{the gain term} - \text{the loss term}$$
$$M(t) = D(i) \times V(p) \times P(s) - D(i) \times V(l) \times P(l)$$

This can be simplified to be:

$$M(t) = D(i) \, [V(p) \times P(s) - V(l) \times P(l)]$$

THE THIRD PRINCIPLE OF ETHICAL POWER

**THE THIRD PRINCIPLE
OF ETHICAL POWER**

Ethical behavior increases the motivation to succeed at task *(t)* because it increases the value of the prize, *V(p)*, and the probability of success *P(s)*, while reducing the value of the loss, *V(l)* and the probability of the loss, *P(l)*.

This has huge implications for how businesses are run. If you run a business where the bearers of bad news or people who express dissenting opinions lose their jobs, then you won't get the bad news early and people won't be willing to express or try out many new ideas. Every business needs a safe environment where people can share even stupid ideas without fear of reprisal. Loss potentials are demotivating. In business and our personal lives, even put-downs represent a loss — a loss in self-esteem. Avoid put-downs.

Similarly, in a sales environment, if you can structure your proposal so that $V(l)$ is low or zero, then you have really dampened or eliminated the loss impediment to the customer's motivation to buy. This is why Sam Walton adopted the strategy of unconditionally guaranteeing every product sold. "Satisfaction guaranteed" became the slogan. This is also why projects that are divisible, testable, incremental, and reversible make so much sense and have a better chance of being sold than those that aren't or can't.

Dreams, on the other hand, increase human motivation by giving us tasks of high value to pursue. As a leader you must get your people focused on a beautiful vision of the future so the value of the future prize of continued employment with your firm is high, e.g., higher incomes and a richer work experience.

People who have a dream and can sell a dream will have a lot of people lined up to deal with them, provided they have capability — the capability needed for people to believe that the probability of realizing the dream is, if not high, then at least is positive, however low. We want to believe, but we want true beliefs. We want dreams that could come true. We want to be part of something significant. We want to give the probability of success for our dreams a high value. Great leadership helps us do that.

Great leadership helps us understand what is possible by laying out a plan we can understand with inputs from us. Step by step, test by test, they bring the future to us.

Whenever possible, good leaders conduct their business on or near the frontier of everyone's existing experience and capability so the chances of success are good and potential losses are small. Losses are demotivating — potential losses are as well. When the probability of losses is low *and* the value of the loss is low, then there is very little to demotivate us. The power of a test market for a consumer product comes from reducing the possibility of future losses. You do the test so that if there a loss, then the loss is confined to the test as opposed to a national roll-out, i.e., you haven't invested $300 million in a national roll-out, for example, but much less in the case of the test market. If we fail in test markets, it doesn't blow our business up, destroying our jobs or our careers, and the shareholder's investment.

This combination of the low value of the loss and the low probability of the loss, in combination with the high probability of success and the high value of the prize, gives us the highest motivation to achieve at the task at hand.

From all of this we see that our motivation depends on the value of gains and losses and the probabilities of gains and losses. Unfortunately, when we are working for people that lack integrity, the value of the job erodes in our minds, because the quality of our work life deteriorates, and further, we never know when we are going to be terminated, possibly wrongfully. As motivation wanes, we start looking for other opportunities.

As a business leader, you have to make trust-building behavior a priority so that people will not only put a value on their future with *you*, but also so that they will predict success *for the company*. When people believe that they are going to be dealing with unethical people in the future, they also believe their lives are going to be miserable, which of course means the value of the prize of continued employment with your company will be low, as well.

On the other hand, if your people are working in an environment with capable people of integrity, they feel comfortable; they predict good things and stability for the future. They think: I can work with this company, maybe not until retirement, but at least as long as I'm here.

This condition throws off a great deal of energy.

Let's summarize two of the major points that we've made:

1. Business ethics is concerned with the gains and losses we expect to realize through our relationships with others.

2. Because ethics involves our expectations, it necessarily involves not only our predictions concerning an uncertain future, but also how our expectations are borne out by subsequent events. In other words, we enter a relationship expecting a certain gain as a result of that relationship (or, in some cases, a lesser loss).

Unfortunately, subsequent events may not yield what we expect. Under these circumstances we may experience a lesser gain or even a loss. The investing community knows that the price of a stock will fall if a firm posts a quarterly profit gain that is less than expected. For example, if a firm's earnings are up 15 percent and the stock market expected that they would be up 20 percent what happens to the price of the stock? It goes down. We put a lesser value on a company enjoying an earnings growth of 15 percent than we do for a firm growing at 20 percent per year.

It's the same way with our careers. If you go to work for a firm and they tell you in the interviewing process that in three years, if performance is good, you will be a manager, and further, that in twelve years you will be a partner, then you will experience a sense of loss if in three years, you aren't even close to being a manager.

Not only will the expected quality of your life in terms of the work that you are doing not be realized, but in all likelihood, your compensation expectations will probably not have been realized, either. You might have made a commitment on a car or a home or a spouse or a child, relying on that original representation, and when it doesn't materialize, you experience a loss. If you are gainfully employed and you get a raise but its not what you expected, then you also experience a real loss. These losses can have a real affect on us, physically, mentally and emotionally.

Let's make a transition to the dark side of business ethics.

THE PRINCIPLES OF BUSINESS ETHICS

We are now in a position to discuss the following principles of business ethics:

- The Dismal Principle
- The Heuristic Principle
- The Principle of Remorse

**THE DISMAL PRINCIPLE
OF BUSINESS ETHICS**

People will experience losses because of relationships with you.

The sooner you grasp this, the better. You cannot get into a business leadership position without being thrown into the middle of conflicts of interest, unrealistic expectations, broken commitments, unforeseen developments, poor performance, and an enormous level of complexity, that makes such losses inevitable and leadership such a heavy responsibility.

THE HEURISTIC PRINCIPLE
OF BUSINESS ETHICS

Behave in a manner that minimizes the losses other people experience because of their relationship with you, and provide the maximum notification possible that such loss potentials exist or are imminent.

Behavior that minimizes losses and provides ample notice is trust-building.

THE PRINCIPLE OF REMORSE

People of integrity feel badly and show their feelings when others suffer losses.

These principles serve as a prologue to the discussion of trust-building behavior.

5 Trust-Building Behavior

There are five categories of trust-building behavior:

1. Preserve the safety of your associates.

2. Do what you say you're going to do.

3. To the extent that you can, tell the whole story, not merely the truth, and do so as early as possible; limited, however, by the conflict of interest principle.

4. Look out for the interests of others even if you must warn the other parties to an agreement of loss potentials or even take a loss yourself to preserve the interests of the other parties to the agreement.

5. Start early and employ each trust-building behavior.

PRESERVE THE SAFETY OF YOUR ASSOCIATES

The first category of trust-building behavior is really basic: preserve the safety of your associates, not merely in an ergonomic sense, but also in the sense of an accident. Consider the AK Steel Company of Middletown, Ohio, a steel company with the worst safety record in the United States for steel mills during the period of 1991 through 1995. Thirteen workers lost their lives at AK Steel during this period. This basic need was not met.

As a CEO, or as manager of a department, you must be very careful about the safety of the physical working environment, as well as the ergonomic issues. When we talk about safety we don't merely mean physical safety, but mental and emotional safety, as well, including being safe from sexual harassment. We need an environment where it is safe for people to share their ideas without the fear of reprisals, without the fear of put-downs. We need an environment where everyone is treated with respect.

I went into a company as president once, and during my first week I asked a question during a meeting. In response, one of the senior managers threw his pencil in the middle of the table and put his head down, and muttered, "That is the stupidest question I have ever heard." That response was beyond the frontier of my experience. I couldn't contain a smile, but almost everybody around the table remained serious, although one woman had a faint smile creep around the corners of her mouth.

I said to the group, "I can see that this isn't a safe environment." I thought, "This fellow is either a big-time star, because he clearly fears no reprisals from a new president, or he's special in some other way," e.g., a jerk. It was extreme behavior. Subsequent events established both his star quality and his jerk potential.

As part of the safety issues, there is an emotional dimension to safety. In safe environments, people behave in a trust-building manner. People treat each other with deference and respect. In safe environments, people have the opportunity to make comments or to ask the naive question without being put down. Even saying, "please" and "thank you," which seems like a small thing to do, is trust-building. When people are nice as a matter of habit and make cooperating a priority, people feel the power of increased motivation and want to be part of the team because they can feel the human values and integrity of the team.

DO WHAT YOU SAY
YOU WILL DO

The second category of trust-building behavior is to do what you say you are going to do. Unfortunately, it's often difficult to predict the future in an uncertain world where you have limited power. As a result, great leaders are careful about what they commit to do: they don't want to oversell and underdeliver. They will stop short of saying, "We will do X," if there is enough doubt in their minds. They say instead that they are going to consider X and that they will try to have an answer on a decision by a specific date. In other cases, great leaders might say, "I have to run this by the chief financial officer, and it might even require board approval; however, if things go well, I will recommend it." That approach builds trust.

Even the chief executive officer has limited power.

It's doubly important for the CEO not to oversell and underdeliver to associates, customers, vendors or shareholders and erode their trust. People can understand the limits to even the CEO's power.

Notwithstanding limited power, great leaders take responsibility for what happens to the group and what happens to them personally. It's quite maddening when a leader does not take responsibility for his or her group whether it be a small department or an entire business. I once worked for a chairman who would delegate everything and work on nothing himself. When something went wrong, he would blame those in the organization, and of course, when things went badly enough, he would terminate the person next in command or the best available scapegoat. This is not an uncommon practice among people who lack integrity. He would say, "Hey, so and so just couldn't do it. He's a real good guy, but just couldn't cut it. He had bad judgment that wasn't apparent initially, and we had to let him go." This is a trust-eroding thing to observe.

Underselling and overdelivering, in the case of earnings projections, is tricky business, whether we're talking about earnings projections for banks or for shareholders or the investment community. It's a tough tightrope to walk.

If we are not bold enough in our projections, we may not be discharging our responsibility to the shareholders and could make our banks and creditors nervous. If we're too bold, we won't be able to hit our numbers. Unfortunately, we can't avoid the issue. But that's what we're paid to do: improve our businesses, to predict that we can, to model the improvement financially and then do it! The good news is that if you can do it, you'll be paid very well.

In a related manner, people who are concerned about *your* loss potentials will work hard to manage your expectations based on the uncertainty and the limits to their power. Your superiors will often see more than you will. It's hoped that you'll see more than your associates will, as far as the future goes. Great leaders make sure to tell you not only about the beautiful vision of the future, but also about loss potentials and the obstacles that are there. In the interviewing process they might tell you, "This company isn't for everybody. I expect my direct reports to work 50-60 hours a week. Some people don't want to do that and it's OK. We even have people here that don't do it. But for people who are new and who are considering coming in as senior management, that is a basic element of our proposal. Working hard, cooperating, being nice are all part of our proposals, as well."

(Can you imagine putting "being nice" as a requirement of employment? I've had enough challenge with difficult people over the years that I now put these provisions in every employment offer. On this point, once a fellow said, "Be nice? I'm never nice, I'm a tough guy."

I responded, "Well within the limits of your toughness, we want you to be on the nice side. Because if you are too tough on your associates, then you won't fit in. You will demotivate our people, and how you affect the motivation of your subordinates and peers is going to be an element of our evaluation of you.")

To the extent that you can, tell the whole story not merely the truth, and do so as early as possible; limited, however, by the conflict of interest principle.

This is the third category of trust-building behavior.

It's a trust-building thing when people tell the whole story to the extent that they can and they do so as early as possible.

By "to the extent that you can," I mean to the extent of your knowledge at that point in time with the understanding that as new information, including new possibilities, or developments impact the story, then the story will be modified accordingly and as early as possible.

By "limited by the conflict of interest principle," we mean that you cannot share information with people who are not entitled to it or people who could use the information to hurt you or the people or firm that you represent.

What makes telling the whole story trust-building is the desire to minimize the losses other people experience as a result of dealing with us. We want to do that. One of the ways we do that is by sharing with our associates the obstacles and loss potentials that we see for ourselves and for them in the future. This is true whether the subject is promotions, raises, responsibility, or even whether or not their job will exist in the future. This is true, especially, in an environment where the company or department may be downsized or eliminated. These are all the things that we want to share with our associates, as these possibilities present themselves.

The Goal: The Mitigation of Damages

What we want to do is not only minimize the loss, but also give our associates as much time as possible to mitigate their own damages. Imagine that you took that entry-level position that was discussed earlier, and that after twelve months your supervisor came to you and said, "We talked about prospects of making manager at the end of three years. But our business is flat and I'm afraid that manager might not be in the cards for you. Although I can't be sure of this, I wanted to share that with you as soon as I felt that a manager position was becoming less likely. I know that it was a key element in your decision to come to work here." To share bad news with someone early is trust-building, even when your associate is devastated by the news. It is trust-eroding behavior to wait until the three year review and say, "Sorry it didn't work out!" or "You should have figured that out!"

Going Beyond the Truth

It isn't just a matter of telling the truth. It's a matter of go-ing beyond the truth. To talk about the future and the ob-stacles before you that may impair your associate's upward mobility in the company is trust-building. Certainly, the bad news is discouraging, but it's a lot better to share the bad news early than to wait for the third-year anniversary and to tell your associate that there is no promotion on the horizon. By sharing the news early, your associate will have had a year or two to try to find work elsewhere. Cer-tainly by sharing your concerns, you risk losing the em-ployee — possibly a good employee, and in so doing, sub-jecting your firm to the related loss should the employee leave — more on this shortly.

On the other hand, you are demonstrating your concern for your associate, and in so doing you have made his or her job with you more valuable because of your integrity. This word will get around to all of your employees and have a positive effect on them, as well.

I had a situation once where there was just that kind of problem developing. As soon as I sensed it, I went to the employee, who had shared with me his goals for the future in terms of the kind of work and compensation that he was looking for. Because I could see that what he was hoping for and what I could deliver would not be the same, I shared the potential problem with him! I wanted to be straight with him — to share my concern about the situation. I did, and fortunately, he stuck it out.

After some time I reiterated that I was really troubled that we didn't have the opportunity that I thought we were going to have when he joined us. He said, "Hey, I understand, you warned me that this might happen when I joined you and you gave me as much notice as you could. But I like what we are doing here. I like this work. I see what you see, too. This isn't totally news, but I think we are going to come back, and I want to be part of the team. I know you are doing all you can. I know it's not your fault. I want to thank you for being straight with me about what you saw and for sharing it with me early."

When you share things with people early, it gives them time to mitigate their losses if they wish to; so if the loss occurs, it's less of a loss in their minds and in reality, because they have the time to adjust to a different prediction of the future, if they choose to. In that way, they become responsible for their own feelings and you don't become the total object of their disappointment in the same way. People experience an increase in trust because they know that you risked a loss for the firm, and possibly a loss to you personally, in order to allow them the notice needed to mitigate their damages. That willingness to take a loss for their benefit builds trust.

This brings us to the next point.

LOOK OUT FOR THE INTERESTS OF OTHERS

Look out for the interest of others even if you must warn the other parties to the agreement of loss potentials or even if you must take a loss to preserve the interests of the other parties to the agreement.

The fourth category of trust-building behavior is: Look out for the interests of other people. Good people don't want you to make a deal that is bad for you. They want to tell you consequences of what the deal is. They don't want you to make a deal that is different than what you expect. Accordingly, if they sense that you misunderstand a point, they are going to point it out — to test it to see if they or you have misunderstood.

I was in a negotiation which took place over a long period with a man named Dick Townsley, the director of materials management with Cadillac, over a long-term contract to design, engineer and manufacture Cadillac limousines. I had put a provision in a subsequent amendment to our proposal that could have been terrible for us. He took me aside and said, "Louie, you have to take that out." Naturally, he explained why, which I grasped immediately once it was pointed out. (I was trying to protect us against one issue in a way that would have inadvertently created potential major problems for us on several other issues.) We changed it. It was an oversight on my part. Afterward, I thought that Mr. Townsley was the greatest guy I'd ever met. Not only did he save me an embarrassment, but he saved us a potentially huge loss and did not ask for anything in return. In his explanation, he said, "This won't be good for you, and it won't be good for us if you sustain losses on this program." Today, I can't even remember the provision, but I remember his concern and what he did!

In hindsight, Mr. Townsley saved us at least $400,000 by pointing out my oversight and possibly much more. Why did he do it? Didn't the $400,000 benefit we received come out of Cadillac's pocket? In a sense it did. In a sense, through Mr. Townsley, Cadillac bore a $400,000 loss for us that had nothing to do with pricing. But as Mr. Townsley subsequently pointed out to me, his main concern at that time — his responsibility to Cadillac — was to insure that Cadillac had a supplier that was financially viable and well motivated to do the best possible job as a source of supply. Cadillac's interest was to have the quality of products they contracted for delivered on time in the quantities and pricing they needed.

In the grey areas of contracts, potential losses loom which could hurt an important vendor and jeopardize a source of supply. Mr. Townsley didn't want that. Fortunately, Cadillac through Mr. Townsley, was able to help us on that issue without hurting themselves "too badly" in the scheme of things, i.e., they were willing and able to bear that loss potential for us. You might say that on an $18 million development program, a $400,000 loss potential isn't significant but it meant a lot to us.

You cannot over-estimate the impact on other people when you go the extra mile to bear a portion of a loss or point out a potential loss in the negotiations of an agreement for which you have no legal liability to bear.

Examples abound in the performance stage of an agreement where both parties to an agreement overlook something which subsequently occurs. I see this all the time, especially in bonus provisions in agreements with employees. These situations are opportunities for the employer to prove their worth by interpreting the provisions in the most favorable light for the employee. Presumably, the company under these circumstances is in a better position to absorb the "additional bonus" than the employee, especially when the company is doing well and the performance of the employee has been good. Being sloppy about the conditions precedent to paying a bonus to a key employee — for example, a manufacturing manager — erodes trust when it comes time to pay the bonus earned and the bonus is denied for a reason something like, "Although your department did well — the company as a whole did not and we can't pay you a bonus under these circumstances."

Manufacturing costs may have declined 10 percent and throughput be up 25 percent through the efforts of the new manager, but the president of the company did not explain in the interviewing process that the company had to be profitable *and* have available cash before a bonus could be paid. This is not an uncommon oversight, unfortunately.

START EARLY AND EMPLOY EACH TRUST-BUILDING BEHAVIOR

Trust-building behavior is hard work. You must start early, work hard and make trust-building behavior a priority. Unfortunately, trust-building behavior is not calculus. Expect problems!

THE POWER PRINCIPLES

All power and the ability to bring about change is limited, temporary, and uncertain.

Unfortunately, our ability to satisfactorily restore losses in the face of ethical dilemmas is limited not only by the power principles, but also by the ethics — the trust-building and trust-eroding behavior — of the other parties to the agreement. You can't make a good deal with bad people! Accordingly, when you accept the mantle of business leadership you must accept the fact that although others will suffer losses as a result of their relationship with you (the dismal principle of business) — you still must behave in a manner that minimizes the losses other people experience, even unethical people, per the heuristic principle of business, if you are to enjoy the full power of business ethics.

The Three Points on the Graph Rule

In business these five trust-building behaviors all work in combination to build or, if absent, to erode trust. Accordingly, if you start early and work hard to employ these elements, you will exhibit trust-building behavior, notwithstanding limited power. Now that you know what the five trust-building behaviors are, you can plot the trust-building (or eroding) behavior of your associates over time, in accordance with the foundation statement: ethics deal with the gains and losses we experience as a result of our relationship with others. To the extent that we can quantify the gains and losses — potential or otherwise — we can plot them on a graph over time.

The Experience Graph of Trust

We can actually plot the trust-building and eroding behaviors for a person or a firm, as the chart on the following page illustrates.

When Mr. Townsley at Cadillac suggested that I take that provision out of our agreement, his suggestion had a large trust-building component to it, because that provision saved us $400,000. Accordingly, Mr. Townsley's warning (behavior) could have been plotted at the point on the graph where "x" equals the date and "y" equals $400,000. Now, on an $18 million program, that may not seem like a lot of money, but it was a lot of money to us. And there was a real sense in which a lesser person would not have warned us.

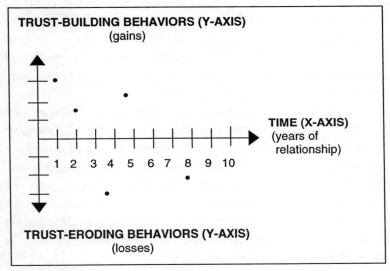

Note: We intuitively plot in our minds the trust-building behaviors (gains) and the trust-eroding behaviors (losses) that we experience as a result of our relationships with others.

When we observe trust-eroding behavior because someone didn't follow through on a commitment, then we would plot that point on the graph on the same basis, except that trust-eroding behavior represents a loss and has a negative value to us and must be plotted below the x axis where y is less than zero.

Remember: points plotted above the line where y is greater than zero represent a gain to us and points plotted below the line where y is less than zero, represent a loss.

This may seem like madness, to keep a trust graph, but mentally human beings all do it whether or not we are conscious of it. When someone cheats on an expense report on a $12 item, it erodes trust!

Naturally, we can't quantify the loss in self-esteem from a put-down, but it is a negative point on the graph and it will be recalled as part of a trust-eroding pattern as future loss points are added to the graph!

Now, some of us are naturally less trusting than others. But normally, when we begin dealing with people we give them the benefit of the doubt for some period of time, not only on issues of integrity, but also on issues related to capability. This period is often called a "honeymoon period." For most of us, something strange happens when through subsequent experience someone gets more than three points on the experience graph that are below the line (i.e., losses) — even if they can't be quantified.

These three loss points represent a bad pattern, unless the person in question has previously established a solid pattern of trust-building in advance, i.e., points above the line in terms of meeting commitments.

We make a mental adjustment regarding a person when we start sensing too many points are being posted below the line, even when the points are not "too far below the line." If these points are close to the line, we may give an additional benefit of the doubt. However, if the points are clearly below the line and are being posted frequently, especially right at the beginning of a relationship, it gets harder and harder to read them charitably, because they are trust-eroding points — points with a negative value to us.

These points below the line affect our motivation because of their effect on our predictions for the future. Such patterns make us nervous as we begin to imagine more trust-eroding points to come — points well below the line that we can quantify, like thousands of dollars of kick backs to a purchasing manager from a cozy vendor.

As an example, I hired a plant manager one time who cheated on his moving expenses, which was a very early point in our experience graph. (Actually, he tried to cheat on a $4,000 "misunderstanding," but was caught by our chief financial officer.) Using this graphical metaphor that my management team is familiar with, the CFO commented, "Hey Louie, that's a point on the graph, isn't it?" Now the CFO had a faint smile, but I didn't — after all, I'd hired the fellow.

I nodded, "Yes."

Three weeks later, another early point was posted when we were discussing a problem and this new plant manager suggested that we solve the problem by telling a lie! It was a ridiculous, unquantifiable and trust-eroding suggestion for everyone in the meeting (about five of us). There was no rationale for it. There was no "higher good" or a potential loss that would or could not be avoided any other way. The truth was perfect. So the CFO looked at me and said, "Hey, that's the second point on the graph, isn't it, Louie?"

So when the third incident quickly followed (I have suppressed what the third incident was), the CFO couldn't wait to get to me. This was the third of three very early points on the graph.

This guy was really bad news. He was capable of telling a lie when the truth sounded better! (He was batting 1,000: 3 for 3.) He had answered the "Can you tell a lie and when would you" questions well in the interviewing process, so this trust-eroding pattern came as a surprise and a real disappointment. In this case, an attempted irregularity on an expense account and a suggested lie in the context discussed, I felt were extreme behaviors. After these two points on the graph, I knew, as my CFO did, we had a bad apple.

My responses to him after both incidents were basically the same: I have found your approach on this to be trust-eroding for the reasons we have just reviewed. You don't see it that way (a lack of remorse), and I respect that and will give you the benefit of the doubt for now. However, trust is a requirement of continued employment here, and should this pattern continue, it will be cause for termination.

Naturally, I put notes in the file documenting the events and our discussion, including the lack of an apology or any indication of remorse which I also regard as a trust-eroding point on the graph. When the third point on the graph came to our attention, then our relationship had come to an end. We all knew it. This fellow turned in his resignation. However, he subsequently filed an age discrimination suit, alleging that he resigned under duress — that we somehow had forced his resignation. His claim was summarily dismissed by the EEOC as we had solid documentation in our file concerning each point on the graph. That is the three-points-on-the-graph rule, and it brings us back to the remorse principle.

THE PRINCIPLE OF REMORSE

When people experience losses because of their relationship with you, even if it is not your fault, it is possible to exhibit trust-building behaviors, given the loss, as follows:

1. **Apologize and mean it.** If you don't mean it, if the apology is not sincere at an emotional level, then don't apologize, because it will not ring true — an insincere apology is in itself trust-eroding.

2. **Exhibit a sense of remorse; feel badly and show it.** People have shock-proof emotion detectors. Few of us can really fake emotion effectively. If you don't mean it, if you don't feel it, then you'll never display it and sustain it properly over time. There is no way. You may be able to do it for a moment, but it quickly wears off. Real remorse is a sustainable emotion — an irrepressible feeling that takes a long time to get out of your system, if ever. Real remorse is reflected not only at the moment but in your future feelings and behavior, not only with that person but with others who will observe you. There is a sense in

which the losses incurred because of the relationship with us remotivates us to work harder and longer in the future to rebuild the trust that may have been eroded, and to do so even if the trust can't be rebuilt.

This brings us to the last rule.

THE FOURTH PRINCIPLE OF ETHICAL POWER

THE FOURTH PRINCIPLE OF ETHICAL POWER

Ethical behavior has an aesthetic quality to it. It is beautiful, and draws us to it and to those who exhibit it.

Trust-building behavior is hard work. For those who are capable of it, it is a priority often an innate priority. They see it as being beautiful in and of itself. Ethical behavior is a triumph of the human spirit, because some people are willing to take a loss for what they believe, even if it means giving up their lives. They want to behave in a trust-building manner for the value it holds for them personally.

They want to be able to look themselves in the mirror and say, "I'm a good person, I like myself." At an emotional level, they have empathy for others, a feeling for other people.

Adam Smith, who wrote *The Wealth of Nations* in 1776, also wrote *The Theory of Moral Sentiments* in 1759 in which he talked about the importance of empathy as an element in ethical behavior and the trust-building equation.

It takes a lot to behave in a trust-building manner. You have to start early and you have to work it hard every day. It's like a garden — if you don't work it every day bad things happen. It's hard enough to deal with things before they mature into problems. It's often impossible to deal with them afterwards.

Unfortunately, per the dismal principle of ethics, people are going to experience real losses as a result of their relationships with you. It's unavoidable.

When you're running a department or a business, in order to exhibit trust-building behavior given that a loss has been incurred, you have to be able to "see" the loss, how *you* or the department or company that you represent is responsible at least in part for the loss. *And* finally, you have to be able and willing to bear the loss, if at all possible! This requires not only empathy for others, but also courage on your part. In addition, you have to run a good department or business, because things aren't always going to work out and if you are running a department or business that's on the financial edge because you're already making losses, you can't take the additional loss for that employee, vendor, or customer, even if you should. Financially, you won't have the ability to take the loss. You won't have room in your budget or the required cash.

In other words, you have to be really tough on the business issues in order to be soft on people. You have to have a good business or run a good department so that you can have a safe environment, an environment where people can feel the trust they need. This save environment will give them the motivation to keep on keeping on when things are tough — and so that you have the wherewithal to take the losses you know you should for those who have suffered losses because of their relationship with you.

Be careful, however, for if you go too far to preserve the interests of the people who report to you, then you may be eroding the trust of your supervisors! Under these circumstances, you can jeopardize your own job or future with the company. As a CEO, if I'm too soft on the issues and not hard enough on the performance of the people, then the board of directors or shareholders to whom I'm responsible may conclude that I have a capability or integrity problem. That's why when I go into a new company, I work very hard to terminate poorly performing managers who refuse to make the effort to improve! By establishing early with my supervisors that I'm really tough on issues of poor performance, it makes it possible to go the extra mile to give the benefit of the doubt to other employees later on as I try to sort out subsequent fairness issues which always present themselves over time.

Ethics is a top-down proposition. The CEO sets the ethical tone of the business, limited by the power that the board or the shareholders are willing and able to exert. The trust-building (eroding) behavior that the CEO exhibits creeps into every area of the business, beginning with the way the CEO says "good morning" and continuing through the decision process. It will get reflected down the line. With the passage of time, the CEO's behavior will become the generally accepted way.

If you find yourself in an environment where trust is eroding or has eroded to a low level, then you must be prepared to suffer your losses — like one trying to ride the back of the tiger. Your other choice is to begin seeking another job opportunity, an exit strategy for you personally.

So far it may appear that we are only reaching for ethics, when in reality, we have spent all of our time talking about building trust in a business relationship.

This is no accident. I have used the concept "building trust" as opposed to "acting ethically" because in an operational sense, I have been much more effective because I employed the concept of "trust-building" behavior, as opposed to "ethical" behavior or "right or wrong" behavior.

People understand gains and losses; what it means to trust another person or not and what trust-building and trust-eroding behaviors are. Whereas the concepts of ethics, right and wrong, duty and obligation are abstractions that are harder to apply.

I have used the concept of "trust-building behavior" in lieu of or as a substitution for "ethical behavior" to avoid this problem.

In a real sense, "trust-building behavior" is not only easier to understand than "ethical behavior," but it is a higher standard, as well.

Is there an ethical standard that requires us to go a little bit out of our way to smile and say "good morning" to an associate and mean it? Or to say "thank you" instead of "thanks," so that an associate can gain an extra bit of self-esteem through our respect?

Of course not, but it is a beautiful thing to do!

The standard of trust-building requires us to go beyond what is specified by agreement, or expected by convention, if we are to enjoy the power and the aesthetic dimension of business ethics.

Good luck!

Index